Prophetic Ministry
Strategic Key to the Harvest

D0973983

Ben R. Peters

Prophetic Ministry: Strategic Key to the Harvest

© 2006 by Ben R. Peters

Published by
KINGDOM SENDING CENTER
P. O. Box 25
Genoa, IL 60135

www.kingdomsendingcenter.org
ben.peters@kingdomsendingcenter.org

ISBN: 0-9767685-8-5

Cover art by Robert Bartow ~ *www.bartowimages.com*
Cover design and book interior by *www.ChristianBookDesign.com*

Contents

Preface

WHEN HARVEST TIME ROLLS AROUND A FARMER KNOWS HIS priorities must be adjusted. He cannot treat a day during harvest like any other day. In fact, even before harvest, he must key into the fact that harvest is coming and spend some time making sure that everything is ready for that significant event.

He studies the condition and progress of the crop. He anticipates when the precious fruit of his labor will be ready to harvest. He studies the weather forecast to see if the weather will be favorable, or if he must bring it in a little earlier to prevent it from being destroyed by heavy rains or early frost, etc.

He makes sure his harvesting equipment is ready. He may use combines, tractors and trucks, and/or other special harvesting equipment, depending on his crop.

He also prepares to hire extra help if he needs it.

The farmer must make sure he has enough room to store the crop in his barns or granaries. He also may need to negotiate with those who will purchase his crop from him, making sure it will find its way to market.

When the time is right he begins the harvest, bringing in the ripest fruit or grain first. He often works very long hours and lets other things go because it is harvest time. Almost anything else must wait because there is often no time to waste. I have seen Canadian prairie farmers working day and night with lights on their combines to get the wheat in before they lose it to rain or heavy frost.

A whole year's income could ride on that brief harvest season. It is the most important time of the year for him as far as farming goes. If he slept through it or went on a vacation then, he would end up without income and lose his farm.

Solomon adds to this truth in Proverbs 10:5, "He who gathers in summer is a wise son. He who sleeps in harvest is a son who causes shame." Children of their Heavenly Father, the Lord of the Harvest, can bring great shame to Him instead of honor just by sleeping during the harvest. Certainly, we don't want to be found guilty of sleeping and missing the incredible spiritual harvest that has already begun.

If we then in the Kingdom of God are entering the

season of spiritual harvest that Jesus talked about, how do we apply what we know about the natural harvest? Are we prepared? Do we know how ripe the harvest is? Is our equipment ready for action? Do we have the personnel that we need? Are we ready to make it a priority and sacrifice other things while we focus on what is crucial for the future?

These are some of the most important questions we need to face in this twenty-first century. The focus of this book is on one of the most important and strategic tools that God has given us to bring in the harvest. That tool is prophetic ministry.

Prophetic ministry is not an option if we want a successful harvest. It is a very necessary part of our harvesting equipment. It is a tool that God has provided for us, and it is a tool we must certainly use if we want to fulfill our destiny and complete our assignment on this earth.

To do God's work, we must use God's tools because He knows what works. We may say, "But I don't know how to use His tools; I'll just use what I'm used to." But the Lord of the Harvest will not honor us using our slow hand tools when He has provided His hi-tech power tools that will accomplish much more in a much shorter period of time. American farmers don't harvest with scythe and sickle anymore. They use the most efficient tools possible.

It's time the church figured out how to use God's

tools and have them ready for the great assignment that God has prepared for us. We are very privileged to be a part of something so exciting in this great hour of history. Let's not miss it! Let's make the most of this awesome opportunity!

Chapter One

Accessing Signs and Wonders Through Prophetic Ministry

FIRST THINGS FIRST

MANY THINGS ARE EASY TO MISS — OFTEN BECAUSE THEY ARE too obvious to be noticeable. I know I've missed more than my share of obvious things. I can be with people and never remember what they were wearing, the color or length of their hair, or any of the other details that people use when they are trying to describe someone they met the night before. These are all the details that my wife and most other folk would clearly remember.

But what surprises me the most is discovering something so obvious in the Scriptures that I have read hundreds of times and have never seen before. The nuggets or secrets that seem to hide the best are the ones you discover when you look at several passages on the same subject that reveal a distinct pattern of repetition or sequential relationship.

One of the most significant nuggets of revelation that I had missed until recently is the simple truth that God's pattern is for prophetic ministry to both precede and prepare the way for the ministry of signs and wonders.

Signs and wonders are extremely important in the plan of God for these final fruitful days of harvest. In doing research for my earlier book, "Signs and Wonders—To Seek or Not to Seek," I discovered that over 90% of all conversions recorded in Scripture came after the unconverted person or group of people witnessed a clear demonstration of the supernatural power of God.

The world is looking for clear proof that God is real. There are so many diverse and different religious groups, all claiming to have "the" truth, that people are justifiably confused and skeptical. There is a deep craving for truth and reality, but most seekers are waiting for something to stand out as the "real thing."

We, as Christians, do have the real thing, but until we use God's power to demonstrate that we have it, most of the undecided will not believe us. And if we are not faithful to use God's tools to do His job, why should they believe us? Or if we are actually "unbelieving believers" (as my friend, Felito, from Mozambique, would describe those who reject miracles), why should they believe?

Our logical reasoning may be better, or make more

sense, than those from another religion, but the satanic spirit of deception on other religions can cancel that advantage. It can never, however, cancel out the pure gospel when the Holy Spirit anoints us and confirms God's truth with signs following, the way God intended for us to preach the gospel, as patterned in Mark 16:20.

I have clearly witnessed the power of signs and wonders to make believers out of skeptics. I have seen thousands of unbelievers, many of them Moslems, become believers when the miraculous healing power of God was demonstrated clearly and conclusively. I have witnessed that power in several countries, including Argentina, Mozambique and to some degree the United States. There are some evangelists with miracle ministries that have seen totally amazing responses to the gospel. German evangelist, Reinhardt Bonke, has recorded over one million souls saved in a single meeting in Africa.

I believe we should earnestly seek God and ask Him to release His power, as He promised to do. He said in Mark 16:17, "These signs will follow those who believe," and in John 14:12, He said, "The works that I do you shall do also, and greater works than these shall you do, because I go to my Father." We must ask Him for rain in the time of the latter rain (Zechariah 10:1), as He instructed us to, if we want to see the harvest.

GOD'S PRIORITIES

But if we truly want to see the miracles to bring in His harvest, then we need to discover and practice His priorities in ministry. Here are the most important priorities that I will try to clarify in the following pages:

1. Pursue intimacy with God and discover the passions of His heart. This intimacy and discovery of His heart will affirm the following steps:
2. Passionately desire to make Him happy. One way to do this (after #1) is to:
3. Zealously desire to build and expand His Kingdom. In other words:
4. Eagerly desire to edify and build His body, to strengthen and equip it to reach the unbelievers with the gospel, confirming the gospel with signs and wonders. The best way to do this is to:
5. Learn how to prophesy and teach others how to prophesy, so that the faith of all believers will grow until by working together, they can:
6. Believe for miracles, and put that faith to work to demonstrate God's love and power.

Let me make something very clear. I am not saying that every miracle is preceded by a prophecy. What I am saying is that prophetic ministry almost always preceded a release of miracles in Scripture. Let's look at a few examples.

EXAMPLES OF THE PROPHETIC PRECEDING THE MIRACULOUS

1. God prophesied the world into existence. He prophesied light and the miracle of light happened.
2. The signs and wonders in Egypt followed God speaking to Moses and then prophesying to the people through Moses and Aaron.
3. The miracles of Elijah and Elisha, like the fire falling on Mount Carmel, and the miracle of Naaman, the leper, being healed, followed their prophetic ministry.
4. Jesus' ministry was filled with miracles, but John the Baptist, who was sent to prepare the way for Him, was strictly a prophet. In fact, the people declared, "John did no miracles, but all that he said of this man was true" (John 10:41).
5. Jesus himself began His own ministry with prophetic declarations and revelations, before He did any miracles (John 1).
6. The New Testament church began with prophetic ministry, followed by many miracles, signs and wonders, just as Joel had prophesied.

7. Amos tells us that God does nothing unless He first reveals it to His servants, the prophets. And everything God does is supernatural. After the prophets proclaim it, God does it. That's His plan, so that He gets the credit for what He does.

A WORD FROM ISAIAH

Isaiah 35:1-6 and beyond gives us a powerful declaration of how to bring about the proliferation of mighty miracles among us.

The first pair of verses prophesy great blessings on the land including that the dead and barren land would become alive and fruitful.

The second pair of verses gives us instructions.

The third pair of verses (5, 6) promise great miracles: the blind will see, the deaf will hear, the lame will leap like a deer and the tongue of the dumb will sing. Then it repeats the promises of verses one and two about the desert becoming alive and fruitful.

What I didn't yet mention is that verses five and six begin with the word, "Then." It is connecting the promises to the commandments or instructions in verses three and four. When we look at these two verses of instruction, we discover that:

THE KEY TO MIRACLES IS PROPER PROPHETIC MINISTRY

Verse three says, *"Strengthen the weak hands and make firm the feeble knees."* In other words, build up the weak. In I Corinthians 14, we discover that prophecy does just that. It is for edification (building up), exhortation and comfort. There may be other ways to strengthen the weak and feeble, but the whole thrust of I Corinthians 14 is how prophetic ministry does that so well.

Verse four is even clearer and is undeniably speaking of prophetic ministry; *"Say to those who are fearful-hearted, 'Be strong, do not fear! Behold, your God will come with vengeance, with the recompense of God. He will come and save you!'"*

When Isaiah tells us to "Say" what God is going to do for someone, he means speak it out or PROPHESY! He told us to prophesy that God will come and save them, even though they were fearful-hearted.

Both verses are totally fulfilled through prophesy in a very clear way. And when we do what verse three and four of Isaiah 35 tells us to do, God promises to do the miracles of verses five and six and beyond.

WHY AND HOW DOES THIS WORK?

Jesus promised that we would do miracles. Then He prayed passionately that we would all be one in Him. His prayers were answered in the early church. They were all in "one accord," and they saw all the miracles that He promised them. Since those days, the church, the body of Christ, has been anything but in one accord, and we see very few miracles. Being in one accord simply means that all the parts of His body are working together for a common goal. The activities of each member are coordinated to achieve the maximum results.

That can happen only when all the parts of the body are trying to help all the other parts of the body, especially the weaker parts. The stronger parts must encourage and strengthen the weaker parts. We often tend instead to criticize the weaker parts because their doctrines are faulty and unscriptural, or they just won't discipline themselves to live the Christian life like they should. Since the body of Jesus is so divided and not as encouraging as it should be, we don't see blind eyes opened and the deaf hear, etc., like we want to.

But when we do strengthen the weak hands (those tired of serving) and make firm the feeble knees (those tired of their journey), THEN they will become a working part of this body and Jesus will have a strong body to work through once again. That body, strong and healthy, will do great exploits for the Father as Jesus did in his body on earth and through the early church which fulfilled Isaiah 35:3, 4.

THE MINISTRY PATTERN OF JESUS

Probably over 99% of Christians are not aware that Jesus did not begin His ministry with the physically supernatural, like turning water into wine (His first miracle), raising the dead or cleansing the lepers. His ministry began when He called His disciples through prophetic words of knowledge and prophetic visions and commands. The book of John makes it clear that Jesus used His prophetic gifts to first make believers of His own disciples and then to also bring most of the city of Samaria to hear Him and recognize Him as the Messiah.

Actually, even before Jesus began to draw His disciples to Himself through prophetic ministry, his relative, John the Baptist, began prophesying Jesus' arrival and ultimately convinced his own disciples to leave him and follow Jesus.

When Jesus came on the scene in John, chapter one, He prophesied to Peter, Philip and Nathanael. He used prophetic knowledge, prophetic visions and prophetic commands to make believers out of them. One by one, including Nathanael, the skeptic, the prophetic gifting made believers out of them and prepared them for the more powerful miracles.

In John 2, Jesus began to do miracles, including turning water into wine. The result is that many more believed in Him.

In John 3, Nicodemus declared that Jesus had to be sent from God, because no man could do the miracles that Jesus did without God's power.

In John 4, Jesus met the Samaritan woman, and with one prophetic word of knowledge and some teaching, He brought her to a place of faith in Him as her Messiah. Then, through her excited testimony about what Jesus had spoken prophetically to her, many Samaritans from that town became believers in Jesus.

After that episode, John 5 records numerous amazing miracles that caused many more people to believe in Him. But clearly, it all began with prophetic ministry to His disciples, and it was followed up with prophetic ministry to the Samaritan woman.

PROPHECY PROPELS APOSTLES INTO POWER MINISTRY

The familiar Acts 2 story and Peter's interpretation of what took place contains some widely undiscovered nuggets of truth. When Peter quoted from Joel about God pouring out His Spirit in the last days, I always read it as a great list of different things that would happen when God poured out His Spirit. Just recently, the veil was lifted from my eyes to see at least one important truth in the passage quoted from Joel.

That simple truth is that everything Peter quoted from Joel had something to do with prophecy. Let's look at it right now.

Acts 2:17; "And it shall come to pass in the last days, says God, that I will pour out of My Spirit on all flesh; Your sons and your daughters shall prophesy, your young men shall see visions, your old men shall dream dreams."

FOUR RESULTS OF THE OUTPOURING OF THE HOLY SPIRIT

First Result—Prophecy

The first result of God's Spirit being poured out on all flesh is that our children, young and old, will prophesy. That's pretty clear, and it's pretty awesome. If He pours out His Spirit upon all flesh, it sounds to me like it's possible for all of our sons and daughters to prophesy. I like that, and I see it happening in our own children—all five of them, plus many spiritual children.

We must also connect Peter's quote from Joel with what was actually happening. Peter began his statement saying, *"This is what was spoken by the prophet Joel."* What did the "this" refer to? It referred to everyone speaking in different languages. Peter is clearly stating that the speaking in tongues in the languages of the people was actually prophetic ministry. This is also confirmed in the early verses of I Corinthians 14, which say that tongues with interpretation is the same as prophesy.

In this case, the tongues needed no interpretation as they were interpreted by the hearers. At any rate, we see that before any other mighty miracles took place, other than the sounds of wind and the tongues of fire, the first miracle that touched the unbelievers was the prophetic miracle of speaking in tongues.

Second Result—Prophecy

The second result is that young men will see visions and old men will dream dreams. This, of course, sounds like something different than prophesying. But wait a minute! When God spoke to Aaron and Miriam in Numbers 12:6, He declared, *"If there is a prophet among you, I, the Lord, make Myself known to him in a vision, and I speak to him in a dream."*

Visions and dreams are sources for prophetic ministry. So far everything quoted from Joel is about prophecy. Let's look at the next result.

Third Result—Prophecy

Acts 2:18 says, *"And on my menservants and on My maidservants I will pour out My Spirit in those days; and they shall prophesy."* Again like the first result, there is no need for explanation. When God pours out His Spirit on our servants (or employees, or whomever), they will prophesy. It happened with Moses and his elders, and it happened with Saul and his messengers when the Holy Spirit fell upon them. It is the most normal first thing to happen when the Holy Spirit comes in His power.

Fourth Result—Prophecy

The fourth result, like the second requires a little explanation. First look at verses 19 and 20. *"I will show wonders in heaven above, and signs in the earth beneath: blood and fire and vapor of smoke. The sun shall be turned into darkness and the moon into blood, before the coming of the great and awesome day of the Lord."*

An anointed friend of ours in New Mexico helped me to see this one. Signs and wonders are messages from God. After all, what is a sign if it has no message? It is no longer a sign. And a wonder communicates the awesome power of God, even though you may "wonder" at first what it means.

And what is prophecy by the way? Prophecy is God communicating a message to man through some means. Therefore it is easy to see that signs and wonders also fall in the general category of the prophetic.

TWO RESULTS OF PROPHETIC MINISTRY

First Result of Prophetic Ministry—SALVATION

Acts 2:21 follows the above passage and says, *"And it shall come to pass that whoever calls on the name of the Lord shall be saved."* This verse should not be detached from the preceding verses that tell us about the coming of the Holy Spirit and the resulting prophetic ministry. The first thing that happens is Prophetic Ministry. The result is that people call on the Lord and are saved.

Second Result of Prophetic Ministry—MIRACLES

After Peter's explanation to the people, three thousand cried out and asked how to be saved. After they were baptized and introduced to the fellowship of believers in Jesus, we read that *"... fear came upon every soul, and many wonders and signs were done through the apostles" (Acts 2:43).*

We finally got to the point of proving our point. Prophecy preceded the miracles again in the early church. It was a powerful example of prophecy, and it could be called group prophecy when everyone was hearing staright from heaven and prophesying at once to different people.

Result of Miracles—MORE SALVATIONS

After the above record that many signs and wonders were done following the first prophetic ministry on the Day of Pentecost, Luke, the writer of Acts, records the healing of the cripple at the Temple gate. Following that healing and the events that it precipitated, we read again that many more of the people became believers in Jesus and the number grew to about five thousand.

Thus we have God's Golden Cycle. Prophetic ministry produces salvation of unbelievers and prepares the way for the more powerful miracles. Those miracles open the eyes of the spiritually blind and produce stronger faith for salvation.

VERY IMPORTANT ANALYSIS
OF ABOVE CONCLUSIONS

Could it be true that *if we are not faithful to properly use the prophetic ministry that God has given to us, we might actually be holding back the mighty signs and wonders that we seek from God?* I do believe there is a lack of miracles in the church resulting at least partly from our failure to obey Paul's commands in I Corinthians 14 to pursue and earnestly desire prophetic ministry.

Prophetic ministry breaks the ice of unbelief and sets the stage for miracles. It also strengthens the whole body of Christ, which gives the Holy Spirit a stronger and more united body to work through.

Without seeking to bring guilt and condemnation, could I suggest that most of us in the western church are not even pursuing signs and wonders, let alone prophetic ministry? We haven't been aware how important miracles are as catalysts for conversion, even as we have been ignorant of how valuable prophetic ministry is for building the body of Christ. It's usually not until we need a healing or a financial miracle for ourselves or our loved ones that we earnestly go after God's miracle power.

Could it be that we typically spend very little time and energy praying for revival and the miracles that could be used by God to light revival fires? In other words, instead of being passionate for what is on God's heart, have we been taught to be "Christian consumers?" Have we learned how to get the best deals from our Supplier, without feeling any obligation to find out what our Supplier or Provider would want from us? I'm afraid the honest answer for a majority of western believers would have to be "yes."

The great news is that God is raising up a strong new generation of prayer warriors and worshippers that are asking for His heart and pouring out their souls in intercession and devotion to their God. They are also seeking Him for His power and asking Him to make them a voice to the nations. They are obeying the command of I Corinthians 14 to "Desire earnestly to prophesy."

This new generation of worshipping warriors is made up mostly of youth, but many of our "older" generation are joining them and spending time in houses of prayer and in personal "prayer closets" crying out for God's will to be done on earth as it is in Heaven. We have no other options if we want God to receive His full harvest.

But we must not forget that we have a command to obey and a pattern to follow.

The command is to desire earnestly or passionately to prophesy.

The pattern is simply to do first things first—that is:

First, prophesy faithfully, encouraging every weak and feeble member of the body, helping them to become contributing members of the body of Christ.

Second, speak prophetically to the lost to bring them to Jesus.

Third, be the body of Christ, working with believing believers to produce the miracles that will convince even the skeptics and reveal the love and power of God to the whole world around us.

Now let's say it even more concisely:

1. Prophesy to Christian brothers and sisters.
2. Prophesy to unbelievers.
3. Produce signs and wonders.

Let me end this chapter with a very contemporary story shared with us by our friend, Surprise Sithole, International Director of Iris Ministries, Mozambique. On a visit to Saudi Arabia, four ladies showed up at the door of his host wearing the traditional garb and head coverings. As he came down the stairs to meet them, the Spirit of Prophecy came upon him, and he prophesied over them revealing and interpreting the dreams they had had.

The prophetic words created faith for salvation for the four ladies. The next day the four ladies brought four couples, all wealthy foreigners living in Saudi Arabia. All four of these couples were converted as a result of the first prophetic words.

Next Surprise was invited to the incredible mansion of a man dying from diabetes. His whole family of eleven children, eleven stepsons and stepdaughters, and many grandchildren and other family members were present. The man was healed after prayer and the whole extended family was converted, even though they were in the heart of the capital of the Islamic religion.

In contrast, many Christian marketplace missionaries have worked in Arab countries, such as Saudi Arabia for many years with almost no conversions. They are to be commended for their sacrifice and dedication, but they have an extremely difficult and discouraging task without a manifestation of the supernatural power of our supernatural God. The solution of course is to practice listening to God's voice on behalf of others, and ask God for the ability to encourage others with a prophetic anointing. Miracles will follow the prophetic ministry and conversions always follow miracles.

Chapter Two

Why is Prophetic Ministry So Important?

A FEW YEARS AGO WE VISITED A LARGE CHURCH THAT WAS HOSTING a well known speaker. In his introduction, the speaker complimented the pastor as being the kind of man you would want to hang out with. Then he made a comparison to people he knew as prophets. He stated that being around a prophet about once a year was plenty, but he could hang out with this kind of a pastor every day of the year.

I do understand the fact that a number of people, who may call themselves prophets, have strange personality traits and they might make people a bit uncomfortable. Some of them may just have very poor people skills. They are sometimes so focused on the message that they don't consider the feelings of the people they are speaking to.

In addition, people can be nervous around prophets, thinking that their secret sins and past failures might be an open book in the eyes of the prophet. Unfortunately, some prophetic people have seemingly enjoyed using prophetic knowledge to expose people's sins, and at times they have done it publicly. This practice and other abuses of prophetic knowledge have hindered the acceptance of this vital ministry.

But for the Kingdom of God's sake, let us never throw out the baby with the bathwater. Prophetic ministry is not designed by God to be an occasional supplement to the pastoral ministry or any other ministry. My extensive research on the gifts and ministries in Scripture reveals that there is no ministry as common or dominant throughout biblical times as the prophetic. From Genesis to Revelation we find prophets and prophetic activity.

In my second printed book, "The Dynamics of Biblical Prophetic Ministry," I recorded my research into the comparative use of the "five-fold ministries" throughout Scripture. After adding up the clearest references to the prophetic and the prophet, as well as apostles, evangelists, pastors and teachers, I discovered that there were three times as many references to the prophetic as there were to the other four ministries combined.

There are so many affirmations in Scripture that God places a high level of importance on prophetic ministry, not to exalt a person or group of people, but for other specific reasons. Let's look at three of the major reasons that God has ordained prophetic ministry in the church.

1. GOD IS A COMMUNICATING GOD

The first recorded activity of God was speaking. God said, "Let there be light." When God created man, He created Him with a special purpose, which was chiefly to provide fellowship for Him with created beings made in His own image. Fellowship requires communication.

The old Hymn, "In the Garden," has a chorus which states, "And He walks with me and He talks with me, and He tells me that I am His own; and the joys we share as we tarry there, none other has ever known." This hymn was considered by one of my seminary profs as not worthy of singing in church because it was too sentimental and not sufficiently substantive. What a sad perspective! There is nothing more important to God than that we walk and talk with Him.

Prophetic ministry is important to God because it is a means of walking and talking with us. Although the full relationship that God had with Adam and Eve in the Garden of Eden is not yet fully restored, He can still communicate personal and intimate things with His children on the earth. He can't fully reveal Himself and His glory to us in our fallen human form. But He can bless us with frequent encouragements, comforts and instructions, if He can find prophetic vessels that are listening and willing to be used in this manner.

We in the western world have access to Bibles in a multitude of translations. God's written "Logos" should be our primary source of edification, exhortation and comfort. But God has clearly designed prophetic ministry to give individuals intimate and confirming revelation from God in response to the current attacks of the enemy on their spiritual lives. The prophetic gift, when it is genuinely anointed by God, brings people a "rhema" word from God, which according to Romans, is a source of faith: "Faith comes by hearing, and hearing by the word (rhema) of God."

What about the argument that we don't need prophecy because the Bible is now complete, whereas the early church didn't yet have the New Testament? There are many arguments to refute this thesis. One of these is the fact that God doesn't withdraw His gifts; not from individuals, and not from His people. "The gifts and callings of God are irrevocable" (Romans 11:29).

In seminary, I did a Greek exegesis on Ephesians 4:11-16, which is the passage that lists the five ministries known as the "five-fold ministries." From the grammar I concluded that all five were given until we come into perfect unity. They are still needed for building up the body of Christ so He can have a strong and healthy body to work through.

Besides the above arguments, and others which we could bring up, I would suggest that any doctrine that puts God in a box of our own making is an abomination to God. In other words, a doctrine that says that God can't still speak to us, because He wrote the Bible for us, is trying to "gag" the One who IS the Word of God. Who is man to tell God when and how He can speak?

Yes, God wrote an awesome book that has blessed the church for almost two thousand years, but that doesn't mean He can't speak in any other way any more. I've written a few books myself, but I still get to speak to people in meetings and conferences. I would argue strongly with anyone who would try to tell me that I don't have the privilege of speaking to people anymore, and I think God would reject that limitation as well. God has never put Himself in our limiting box and He never will.

Did we not hear the voice of God calling us to repentance? Have we not heard His still small voice giving us comfort and conviction? Has He not prompted us to speak or to give or to comfort, etc.? All of the above are examples that God is still speaking to us. And we must not draw an arbitrary line that says God can go so far in speaking to us, but no farther.

This is much like the argument for miracles. Many people believe that salvation is the greatest miracle, which most of us would agree with. But why can't

God do lesser miracles for us, if He can do the greatest miracle? It really makes no sense at all.

The simple truth is that this doctrine, called "Cessationism," is the result of man trying to justify the lack of spiritual power in the church. It is also a reaction to those who appear to have an attitude of spiritual superiority. If people seem obnoxious and prideful towards us, we have a built-in inner motivation to prove them wrong.

The desire to be right is one of man's strongest and most controlling motivations. It is a force strong enough to clamp our minds shut to all the facts that are inconsistent with what we believe. Those committed to cessationism will not be easily convinced by my logic or anyone else's, and I don't want to fill up space with my response to the two or three Scriptures they would use to build their case to prove their thesis.

The best way to prove that miracles and prophetic ministry are for today is to let people see genuine miracles and hear true prophetic words. In other words, we need to be so filled with God's love for them and with faith in His power that we find ways to meet their personal needs with the power of the prophetic and the power of the miraculous. When their sick child is healed by the prayer of faith, they will believe in miracles. And when you reveal the thoughts of their hearts in personal struggles and then bring healing to their inner brokenness, they will believe in the prophetic.

We have seen the latter frequently in our own ministry. So many have been brought to our meetings as skeptics, but they left as believers in prophetic ministry. Our friend, Sharon Sherbondy, has shared publicly how she came ready to slip out if we got weird on her. God revealed her heart to her through prophetic ministry and now she is moving in prophetic and healing ministry herself. In addition she has opened doors for us to minister to scores of her friends and associates as well as to many teens, almost all of whom had never experienced prophetic ministry before.

Another friend, Paul Lagerquist, an airline pilot, came with a definite attitude of skepticism, not knowing us at the time. His own testimony is that he came in as a skeptic and left as a believer in prophetic ministry. Together with his wife, Donna, and Sharon Sherbondy, they began a ministry called Trumpet Call, where they practice prophetic ministry and healing among people who previously didn't believe in either. By the way, Donna Lagerquist recently experienced a major miraculous healing herself that followed prophetic words to her confirming that God was going to heal her.

Getting back to the main point we were making earlier, God is a God that loves to share His heart with His people. He loves to walk with us and talk with us. We have seen thousands of people touched by the words that God gives us to share with them. He could choose to speak in an audible voice to them, but He has chosen instead in most cases to use human vessels for that communication. And it makes sense! If we are His body, we should be speaking His words and doing His deeds.

2. PROPHETIC MINISTRY EDIFIES (BUILDS) HIS BODY

Most of us have a very limited view of how important the body of Christ really is to Him. Paul repeatedly declared that the church IS His body. Just as our individual human bodies are important to us, so is His present earthly body important to Him.

Our body does all the work that produces income and other resources for us and our family and others. Even those who work mostly with their minds must use their other physical body parts after their brains process all the knowledge, and logic, etc. If they do not speak it or write it out or somehow communicate it or produce something with it, all the brilliant ideas in their minds will never change anything in their world.

Even so, the body of Christ is the agent that God has chosen to do His work on the earth. Consequently a weak and sickly body will accomplish little, but a strong and healthy body will accomplish much. Therefore, it is extremely important from God's Kingdom perspective that we do everything that He asks us to do to make His body as strong and healthy as we possibly can.

This simple truth is very critical to the focus of this book. We cannot bring in a great harvest if the harvesters are weak and sickly, or if the harvesters' tools are dull or broken. We must listen to what God is speaking to His church and then obey His instructions. What He has already clearly spoken in I Corinthians 14 is that prophecy will edify or build and strengthen His body. He clearly states through Paul in verse 12 that we should seek to excel, or in other words, "pursue excellence" in learning to edify the church.

Prophecy was designed to counteract and preempt the attacks that come from our enemy on every individual member of the Body of Christ. When prophetic ministry has been stifled or eliminated from the church, our enemy has a distinct advantage. Instead of being able to neutralize the fiery missiles, many members of His body find themselves taken out of the battle and the harvest for long periods of time, while they lick their wounds and slowly heal.

On the other hand, when prophetic gifts are properly functioning, no member of His body stays down for long. The Holy Spirit will prompt one or more people to speak life and healing to the wounded, and they are able to quickly get up and get back to their calling and labor for Jesus. Just from our own little ministry, we could point to hundreds of people who needed that little extra nudge from God to encourage them and get them back into their calling and ministry. It is totally amazing and awesome to think about.

3. PROPHETIC MINISTRY PREPARES US FOR FUTURE EVENTS

When God says He does nothing until He has revealed it to His servants the prophets, He is making a powerful statement. If we believe what He says, we will be wise to associate with as many prophets as possible. We have heard true stories of large groups of people being protected from disaster because they listened to a prophet and escaped before it was too late. Most of those who mocked and refused to listen were brutally massacred.

Just today, as I write this in Henderson, Kentucky, I heard the story of a pastor from California, who was told by a man sitting next to him on a plane that he was going to receive three offers that week for his church building. He should pray which one to take because God wanted him to sell it. The pastor had no intention or desire to part with his building, but he told his son who was traveling with him about the man's words to him. The son said, "Dad, there was nobody sitting beside you." The dad had a hard time believing him, but when the three offers came in the next week, he accepted the best offer. The church became a mobile congregation for some time.

Shortly after the sale of the property, the Rodney King riots took place in that very neighborhood. Property dropped in price to a third of its former value. God had protected His own resources by sending a heavenly prophetic messenger. Perhaps God would have sent a human messenger if one had been available and able to hear the voice of the Lord, but in this case it is apparent that He had to use a non-human messenger to speak the prophetic word to this pastor.

The story of Joseph is one of the greatest examples of escaping disaster through listening to prophets. Without Joseph, millions of people would probably have starved to death, but with him there was a great harvest brought in. There was a natural harvest reaped in the seven good years and there was a spiritual harvest as people heard about Joseph's prophetic revelation that saved them from starvation.

The prophet Elisha warned the King of Israel several times when the Syrian army was about to attack, giving the armies of Israel enough warning to be prepared and thwart the Syrian military threat. The King of Syria was convinced that one of his own generals was selling his secrets to the enemy, but he was informed that the prophet in Samaria was broadcasting what the king was speaking in his bedroom.

Daniel read Jeremiah's prophecies that after seventy years the Jews would be able to return to the land of Israel. This revelation stirred Daniel to intercede for his people, resulting in the fulfillment of the word and an abundance of further revelation.

In the book of Acts, a prophet, named Agabus, prophesied a famine in Jerusalem. This knowledge allowed others in the church at large to help the believers in Jerusalem and prevent their starvation.

Paul's prophetic warning was ignored by the captain of the ship taking him to Rome, and they all suffered shipwreck as a result. When he gave them more prophetic advice during the storm, they all listened and were spared further suffering.

For years I have proclaimed to whatever audience God had given me that the most valuable thing we can have in difficult and perilous times is the ability to hear God's voice. No one but God knows what is coming on the earth, and only those who can hear His voice can prepare us for whatever is about to happen on this planet.

4. PROPHETS ARE NEEDED TO FULFILL LEADERSHIP ROLES

God is clarifying the roles of all of the five-fold ministries today and putting them together as a powerful team. For more details, see my book entitled, "Folding

Five Ministries Into One Powerful Team."

The role of the prophet is critical in the bigger picture if we want to bring in God's harvest in a timely manner. The prophet is called to work alongside of the apostle. Together apostles and prophets form the foundation of the church of Jesus Christ, of which He is the chief cornerstone. Apostles depend on the prophets to give them up-to-date words of guidance and insights from Heaven. They need confirmation and wisdom from Heaven as they face major leadership decisions.

Being called the foundation and given the assignment that goes with it, is not an insignificant thing. A foundation determines the shape and size of the structure that is to be built upon it. If the foundation is shallow, the building will not be very tall. If the foundation goes deep enough, you can build a skyscraper on it. If the foundation is a rectangle, the building will be the same. Whatever shape the foundation takes, the building will correspond to it.

The prophet is depended upon by both apostles and other leaders. Evangelists or itinerant apostles may get their marching orders through prophets as they did in Acts 13. Other ministries such as teachers and pastors may be given their calling or at least a confirmation of their calling by prophets. These callings all relate to their part in the harvest. The prophets must be in place to provide clarity and confirmation or affirmation to other members of the team that God is putting together.

Our own ministries have been confirmed many times by prophets that God has sent our way or sent us to. Even as a child, I was blessed with several special appointments that gave me a sense of destiny. As adults, Brenda and I have received some profoundly powerful words to confirm and give hope to us, even in very discouraging times.

The prophet does not have the calling to be a jack-of-all-trades kind of ministry person like we expect of the person we call "pastor." His primary responsibility is to be listening to God. He may be a very weak administrator or teacher or preacher. What we need from the prophet is to know that He is hearing clearly the word of the Lord. We have others who can teach, preach and evangelize. We desperately need those who clearly hear the voice of God.

5. PROPHETIC MINISTRY IS A POWERFUL, BUT OFTEN IGNORED, EVANGELISTIC TOOL

We referred to this in the previous chapter, but we must include this truth again. The end result of all the prophetic signs quoted from Joel by Peter in Acts 2 was that "Whoever calls on the name of the Lord will be saved." One of the main reasons God communicates through the prophetic, builds up His body through the prophetic, and prepares us for future events through the prophetic is so that we will be ready to use this gift to bring in the great harvest.

Prophetic ministry was an evangelistic tool used well by Jesus and also used by the apostles. Today, we see it working time and time again as we and others prophesy to people who have no awareness of how important they are to a loving creator God, who has an awesome plan for their lives. When they hear the "rhema" voice of God speaking to their inner man, they surrender to this loving Savior and become believers.

One of our favorite examples is our friend Cheryl in Calgary, Alberta, Canada. The first time we met her, it was in a small meeting in a basement with young adults, including a couple of chain smokers, making the air pretty thick for us non-smokers. None of them really knew God, except the gal that had been witnessing to them.

Brenda turned to Cheryl and said, "Jesus really loves you!" and then began to share some other prophetic words with her. Cheryl felt the love of Jesus and later declared that no one had ever looked her in the eye before and told her that Jesus loved her. The result was that Cheryl immediately became an evangelist and brought other friends and family members to church and to get ministry from us.

The next time we came to town, Cheryl was getting baptized and sharing her testimony with the church.

Later when we came to the same church again, one of the young men she had introduced to the Lord proposed to her at a Sunday night meeting. We returned again later and they were getting married. If I'm not mistaken we have also witnessed her children being baptized and a baby dedicated, etc.

Prophetic visions and dreams have been used to convert Pharaohs and emperors in Joseph's day and Daniel's day, and they are being used today to bring countless Muslims to the Lord, as well as people of all backgrounds. We have hardly even tapped into this incredible tool for the harvest, but the church is finally becoming more and more aware of its value and how to use it to expand the Kingdom of God on the earth.

Chapter Three

Increasing Prophetic Clarity

TRAINING OUR EARS TO HEAR

PROPHETIC MINISTRY IS ALL ABOUT LISTENING. THE ART OF listening is something most Christians are not very good at. The same holds true in our human relationships. Most of us would rather talk than listen. We all want to be heard, but there are not enough people who want to listen for that to happen.

The problem with prophetic ministry is that it is totally dependent on our ability and desire to listen to Someone that wants to talk to someone who wants to listen. Not long ago, God highlighted a Scripture during a soaking session in Oneonta, New York, with our friends, Danny and Donna Legualt. This verse really jumped out at me.

It was Psalm 81:13, which begins like this: "Oh that My people would listen to Me!" This verse is in the middle of a discussion of the fact that Israel would not listen to their God. He then makes the statement that if they had listened to Him when He spoke, they would have avoided some serious problems and they would have been prospering beyond their wildest dreams. But instead they chose to listen to their own ideas and plans, which led them into disaster after disaster.

When I read this verse, it stood out to me as the statement of a God who was quite frustrated with His kids, like a parent with a teenager that just would not listen to good advice. I really believe God is still saying to His church, "Oh that My people would listen to Me!"

We all have good ideas and lots of wisdom from our experiences, but it can't match the ideas and wisdom of the God who knows the future as well as the past. If we just wanted a good life free of major problems and full of major blessings, it would be a great idea to learn to listen to God. But if we want to be useful to Him in the process of bringing in the great final harvest of souls, it is not just a good idea to learn to listen to His voice, it is absolutely and totally essential.

We have established the fact that God is a communicating God and that He does speak to us today. We have just seen that He is looking for people who are willing to listen to Him. So the next important step is discovering how to increase our capacity to hear His voice.

HELPFUL SUGGESTIONS

1. Listen for the Rhema While You Read the Logos.

The logos is the eternal written word of God found in Scripture. It is historically accurate and abides forever. The rhema is usually interpreted as a word that comes alive in a particular situation or time for a particular person or group of people. It is personalized and specific. It is the rhema word that produces faith. "Faith comes by hearing, and hearing by the word (rhema) of God." (Romans 10:17).

I have heard the rhema in the logos hundreds or thousands of times. The Bible has been my chief source of prophetic input. God speaks personally to me through words that were written to speak to millions of readers throughout thousands of years. But it's like that verse was written just for me and I hear God speaking to me through that verse.

If you want to develop clarity in hearing God's voice, I suggest that you get familiar with His Logos, while listening for His Rhema as you read. This will provide you with an invaluable protection from error. Knowing God's eternal, unchanging Word will protect you from deception from the enemy or your own flesh. The Bible is our standard. Every word must conform to His eternal word.

While you listen for the rhema in your reading of the Bible, you will be developing the ability to hear His voice in your spirit. That ability will help you to recognize His voice when you are with other people and He wants to download some specific information for them.

2. Spend Time Soaking With Worship Music in His Presence

While my personal journey has been one of being saturated in the Bible, my wife's journey has focused more on soaking in the presence of Almighty God while listening to her favorite worship music. Together, we can bring a balance to each other. I have more Bible knowledge to affirm or adjust her input, and she has a greater sensitivity to spiritual activity in the invisible realm. When we listen to each other, we can receive confirmation that we are truly hearing accurately from God.

Soaking is really a simple, yet profound experience that all of us can do, if we value the ability to hear God's voice. Soaking, however, may seem to some of us like a waste of time. Why just lay there listening to music when we could be studying, writing sermons or getting out there preaching and teaching? That, of course, is a

Martha spirit manifesting out of our religious heritage. A lot of things that God asks us to do don't make sense to the carnal mind, but if we want a Mary spirit that pleases Jesus, we will want to just sit at His feet and learn to listen well to what He has to say.

Listening requires discipline. We must stop trying to figure everything out and rest our minds to listen. Many of us have a hard time doing this. I am very guilty of wanting to talk more than listen. I have often found myself, while in conversation with others, thinking of what I will say when the other person stops talking, rather than truly listening to what my companion has to say. I fear we do that far too much with our God. We must discipline our minds to stop our own thinking and focus on listening.

Music Helps to Quiet Our Minds

Music can provide a perfect environment for us to hear God's voice more clearly. Music soothes the troubled spirit. King Saul's advisors understood that when they brought David in to play his harp. David's anointed worship music brought peace and rest to Saul's spirit. Anointed worship can quiet the confusion of competing voices in our own spirit and allow us the freedom to listen to the voice of God.

Music Can Be a Vehicle Into the Spirit Realm

Music that is inspired from Heaven can also be a vehicle to transmit the voice of God to the prophetic ear. Elisha called for a minstrel to play when the king needed a strategic plan for the battle he was facing. As the minstrel began to play, Elisha received a prophetic download from Heaven, and Israel was spared from defeat by their enemies because they had received the strategy from God, Himself (II Kings 3:15).

When we spend time soaking with worship music, we are becoming familiarized with heavenly frequencies and we can easily recognize them as friendly voices. As we have often heard, when people working in banks handle lots of genuine money, it is easy for them to recognize the phony. The more they handle the real, the more sensitive they are to the difference when the counterfeit appears. By the same token, the more we hear the voice of God, the easier it is to recognize a different voice as not the voice of God.

Jesus said, "My sheep know my voice. They won't listen to the voice of a stranger" (John 10). The disciples must have listened to the voice of Jesus for hundreds of hours. Later it was said that their wisdom and boldness was attributed to the fact that they had been with Jesus. He was gone from them physically, but they were still hearing His voice and they could distinguish it from the voice of the religious leaders of their day. They knew that they must heed the voice of God rather than the voice of men.

Waiting on the Lord

Most Christians know well the final verse of Isaiah 40. It reads, "But those who wait on the Lord shall renew their strength, they shall mount up with wings as eagles; they shall run and not be weary, they shall walk and not faint" (Isaiah 40:31). And most Christians have heard messages on the concept of eagles molting the old feathers and being provided with new ones. That is the picture of renewing their strength.

But I'd like to point out another very significant application of "waiting on the Lord." Mounting up with wings like an eagle can easily be seen as a reference to rising up into the spirit-realm with our spirit and seeing with the "eagle-eyes" of the prophet.

I strongly believe that waiting on the Lord produces prophetic vision and insight. The eagle can see what humans cannot see. They can see clearly from a much greater distance. And they can see from a heavenly perspective as opposed to seeing things from ground level.

Waiting on the Lord is very similar to soaking. It involves three distinct actions that I can illustrate from a very familiar scenario:

You probably eat out in a restaurant from time to time with friends and family. When you do, almost without fail, someone will come to your table, greet you with a smile and ask what he or she may do for you. If you don't get that kind of service, you will probably complain to the manager or just not come back to that restaurant.

The person who comes to serve you is said to "wait on you" and is called a waiter, waitress or waitperson, depending on how politically correct you want to be. There is a difference between waiting "for" someone and waiting "on" someone. We are told to both wait "for" the Lord and to wait "on" the Lord.

It's waiting on the Lord that produces the "eagle eyes" of the prophetic ministry. Waiting on the Lord is illustrated by the actions of the person sent to serve you in your favorite restaurant.

1. **They Listen:** First the person comes and asks you what he or she can do for you. Then they listen carefully to what you have to say, making notes and being careful not to make a mistake.

2. **They Obey:** Secondly, the person does his or her best to fulfill your wishes, by presenting your request to the kitchen and bringing bringing you exactly what you ordered. They do this with a sweet attitude, knowing that in honoring you, they will also be blessed.

3. **They Thank You:** After they serve you they thank you for coming in and allowing them to serve you.

Now let's apply these three steps to waiting on the Lord.

1. **We Listen:** We come into His presence with a humble heart asking Him how we can serve Him today. We are honored with the privilege of serving Him. Then we listen carefully to what He has to say to us. He shares what is on His heart at that moment.

2. **We Obey:** When we listen well to His voice, we will hear the burden of His heart and we will know His desires. In the process of waiting on Him, we hear Him saying to the hosts of Heaven, "Whom shall we send and who will go for us?" It is our great joy then, like Isaiah, to say with childlike passion, waving our hand to be noticed, "Pick me, Jesus! I want to go for You! Let me be Your messenger." He gives us more instructions and sends us on our way with His blessing.

3. **We Worship:** When Jesus, through the power of the Holy Spirit, uses us to touch someone's life, transforming them in a wonderful way,

we may be easily tempted to entertain the thought that we are quite anointed and other people must have noticed how powerful our ministry was in that moment. This is when we must do the only proper and safe thing to do. We must bow down and worship the Lord for the wonderful opportunity to serve Him. We acknowledge that it was only through His mercy and grace that He used us like He did. Worship refocuses on Jesus and takes our eyes off ourselves.

L. O. W. – Listen – Obey – Worship. The key to waiting on the Lord is getting LOW before the Him in humility and to serve him by Listening, Obeying and Worshipping.

The results of waiting on the Lord are:

1. Downloading His strength
2. Developing Prophetic Vision

These are powerful keys to developing clarity in prophetic ministry. Try applying them a little more each day, until you begin to see breakthroughs in your ability to hear and recognize God's voice, especially for others in need of your encouraging words.

Chapter Four

Overcoming the Fear of Prophetic Evangelism

As WE TOUCHED ON EARLIER IN THIS BOOK, ONE OF THE KEY purposes of prophetic ministry is to convince the unbeliever that God is real, God knows and loves them and He is willing to forgive them and use them in powerful and wonderful ways. The problem most Christians face is the same problem that the "apprentice apostle," Timothy, faced as a young man being mentored by the senior apostle, Paul.

The problem Timothy had with using his spiritual gifts was the problem of timidity or fear. Let's look briefly at II Timothy 1:6, 7, which will be the focus for much of the teaching in this chapter.

"Therefore I remind you to stir up the gift of God which is in you through the laying on of my hands. For God has not given us the spirit of fear, but of power and of love and of a sound mind."

First of all, chances are you didn't know that these two verses were back-to-back in Scripture. I have surveyed many congregations and less than 1% of the people knew what verse preceded verse seven. Most people know that God has not given us a spirit of fear, but almost no one knows that this verse was in the context of using spiritual gifts.

As we have discovered in our research on spiritual gifts, prophetic ministry is the most dominant ministry by far throughout Scripture. It is highly likely, knowing how Paul admonished people to desire the gift of prophecy, that Paul had also encouraged Timothy and perhaps imparted this gift to him with the laying on of his hands.

Another reason that he may well have been talking about the gift of prophecy is that it is a gift that requires speaking out and speaking for God. Most people are afraid to speak out in public and especially if they are expected to speak for God. Surveys have shown that the number one fear of man is speaking in public. The number two fear is the fear of death. This confirms the statement that people would rather die than speak in public.

Prophetic ministry can be scary, and because it has been abused by people who have taken advantage of the power it wields, many are not open to its use. Therefore, it can be a challenge to get started prophesying. Like Timothy, we easily get attacked by a spirit of fear.

So what must we do to overcome that fear of speaking

out the word of the Lord, especially to those who don't know God and may mock or reject us if we open our mouth and try to represent the Lord and His words? The following steps based on the above verses will help us when we prophesy to anyone, but especially when we are speaking the word of the Lord to a non-believer.

WHEN FACED WITH A PMO (PROPHETIC MINISTRY OPPORTUNITY) DO THE FOLLOWING THINGS:

1. Rebuke the Spirit of Fear

The spirit of fear attacks everyone, but it can get really annoying when you want to serve God with the gifts He gave you. Our enemy hates these gifts because he knows how powerful they are and that he has no power to withstand them. Like Moses' serpent, they always trump his serpents, no matter how many there are.

The enemy's only defense is to bring fear to thwart your attempt to use your gifts for the Kingdom of Heaven. If he can do that, he has prevented you from bringing about some serious damage to his kingdom.

We have experienced countless attacks designed to take us out before we use our gifts on important ministry assignments. Brenda has the stronger prophetic gifting, and having had to deal with a lot of fear in her childhood, she has been the target of panic attacks, physical sickness and pain and many other things that have come to keep her from terrorizing the kingdom of darkness.

Of course, when the wicked one can hurt the wife and bring fear on her, he can distract the husband and change his focus from the Kingdom vision to rescuing his ministry partner from the attack of the enemy. Thankfully, Brenda is a real warrior and will not quit or give in. We have fought off the attacks together, and we have missed only a very few opportunities to minister because of physical sickness such as the flu.

The clear truth about what we have seen is that the harder the attack, the greater the meeting will be. And when we see what the enemy has tried to prevent, we are all the more determined to terrorize his kingdom of darkness by bringing in brighter and brighter light. That light is the glory of the risen Christ, who works miracles and heals broken hearts, giving hope to those in despair and resurrecting those who are dead in their spirits.

So when we have a PMO, we are wise to pray out loud or quietly if the occasion requires it, "I rebuke the spirit of fear that wants to attack my mind. It didn't come from God and it has no right in my life. I cover my mind with the blood of Jesus Christ, and I will not believe the enemy's lies, in Jesus' name."

We should continue our prayer with the following points from II Timothy 1:7.

2. Claim the Spirit of Power

I now claim the Spirit of Power, which God has given to me. I have been given an anointing to release His words of life. I have been called to speak as an oracle of God (I Peter 4:11). I have been immersed in and filled with His Holy Spirit to be a witness to Him in all the earth and I will not fear, but be filled with courage and strength in the Lord my God.

3. Claim the Spirit of Love

I also claim the Spirit of Love, for God IS love and He is in me, working through me. I know that love is the only pure motivation for using any gift of the Holy Spirit. I renounce my selfish ambition and pride of gifting. I want no glory from what I am about to release. I only want God to be glorified and His Kingdom blessed. I also want to help this precious person that He loves with an everlasting love. I thank you Lord for the Spirit of Love that flows through me.

4. Claim the Spirit of Sound Mind

And finally, I claim the Spirit of a Sound Mind — a mind that thinks clearly the thoughts of God — a mind that discerns between good and evil, the devil, the flesh and the Holy Spirit. I yield my mind to Your mind, for Your Word says that we have the mind of Christ. And I thank you for these precious gifts, Lord. May I bring you all the glory, honor and praise, in Jesus' name, Amen.

Let's notice how the three positive Spirits of God counteract the negative spirit of fear.

Fear is a feeling that we don't have power to counter the attack that is coming against us. When God gives us the Spirit of Power, the fear is neutralized by the awareness that we have more power than our enemy and it is he who is afraid of us. This gives us the boldness to go on the attack, rather than retreat.

The Spirit of Love also has the power to overcome the spirit of fear. I John 4:18 says, "There is no fear in love, but perfect love casts out fear." How does this work?

Fear that we will be hurt is one force. Love for someone else is another force. When someone we love is really hurting, we lose our selfish focus and disregard what anyone thinks of us. We will do whatever it takes to bring healing to the person we love. Therefore, when God gives us a Spirit of Love for a person, the power of that Divine Love is far stronger than the power of selfish fear. This is the same Spirit of Love that put Jesus on the cross for us. It cannot be stopped by the spirit of fear from our enemy.

Thirdly, the Spirit of a Sound (or healthy) Mind can overpower the spirit of fear. The spirit of fear brings confusion and does not allow us to think logically. It tells us that we will be defeated, disgraced and destroyed. But when we have the Mind of Christ, we realize that God is real, His gifts are real, He loves us, and He has promised great things for us and through us. We realize that greater is He that is in us than he that is in the world. We understand that we are more than conquerors through Him who loved us, and we are ready to do whatever He has asked us to do. Furthermore, we know that He is able to make everything clear and real to us.

Thus the very basis or the foundation of fear has been pulled out from under the spirit of fear, and the fearful thoughts now make no sense to us. Our minds are no longer clouded by fear and uncertainty. Rather, we have a "Blessed Assurance" that God is for us and therefore who can be against us?"

Armed with this incredibly powerful arsenal, we can overcome this dreaded foe with a one, two, three punch. Power, Love and Sound Mind will come to our rescue, demolishing this hindrance to the progress of the Kingdom of God.

MORE HELPFUL ADVICE

1. Be Natural

You don't need to look or sound spiritual or professional. You just need to look and sound like a friend, or someone who cares. If the person you want to minister to doesn't know you, you might just say, "Excuse me, but I feel like God wants to encourage you because you've been having a hard day. If it's OK, I'd like to share what I feel He wants to say to you today."

Brenda's favorite approach is: "God gave me a prayer for you. Do you mind if I share it with you?" Almost everyone says, "Yes." Ask God to give you the words that fit with your personality and the people you approach. He will help you with every detail if you ask Him.

2. Be Humble

Don't try to impress people that you are gifted or powerful. If you try to prove something to others, you put the focus on yourself, not on God, and the enemy has an open door to bring fear into your heart. Instead, come with the heart and attitude of a servant. You are there for them and for Jesus, not to build your self-confidence in yourself. It's only because you humbled yourself to admit you needed Him that He saved you and gifted you. But now you need to remember the verse that says, "Freely you have received, freely give."

When God uses you, be sure to worship Him and give Him the glory for what He has done through you. If people praise you for helping them, just say, "Praise the Lord! He wanted to encourage you so much that He chose to use the nearest person available, which happened to be me."

3. Be in Love with Jesus

Your power over fear will grow as your intimacy with Jesus grows. When you are so in love with Him that you just want to please Him day and night, you lose your concern for yourself and your own reputation. And when your love for Him transfers to those He puts in front of you, you will have little fear because of your focus on your mission to share His love with others. Fear comes from being conscious of our own inadequacy. His love conquers that fear.

Chapter Five

Understanding the Harvest

U P UNTIL THIS POINT, WE HAVE TALKED ABOUT THE HAR-
VEST without defining it. Most Christians just assume
that the harvest means getting unsaved people saved,
or making believers out of unbelievers. Getting people
saved is a necessary part of the harvest, but it is not the
harvest in itself.

If we think about the natural harvest, it is very clear
that harvesting is not really the conversion of something
into something else. For instance, it is not changing tares
into wheat. Tares remain tares and are burned; wheat
remains wheat and is taken into barns. While the grain
is growing, it is simply immature grain, but when the
grain is mature and ready it is taken from the stalk and
brought into the farmer's barns.

DEFINING HARVEST

What then really is the harvest? The harvest is taking the fruit or grain from the plant that it grew on and then gathering it together into a safe place for the master to use. Thus the harvest is not actually the conversion of souls, but the taking of them out of their past environment and then the gathering of converted souls into the security of the barns of the Master where they are available for the Master's use.

The harvest is also the reward for previous labor, including your own, that of others and God's. That labor involves cultivating, sowing, watering and weeding. As Jesus said, "The seed is the Word." Nothing can be harvested unless someone has sown a seed that has germinated and matured. Harvest is the joyful result of a seed that has produced new grain.

The Lord knows who the tares are and who the wheat is. People will choose for themselves, but God already knows how they will choose. He has been helping them grow into their destiny as His sons and daughters since they were born. When we present the gospel—the good news—to them, we may be just sowing the first seed or we may be putting in the sickle to reap the ripened fruit, which grew after someone else sowed the first seed.

SCATTERED SHEEP—RIPE HARVEST

Jesus had compassion on the multitudes of Jews because they were scattered like sheep without a shepherd (Matthew 9). Then He told His disciples how ripe the harvest was, but that there was a shortage of laborers in the field. He was talking about His own people, the Jews. He also declared that He wanted to gather the people of Jerusalem together like a chicken with her chicks, but they were not willing (Luke 13:34).

"Scattered" is the opposite of "gathered." God always wants to gather, while the enemy wants to scatter. We are safe when we are gathered in one place, but much more vulnerable when we are scattered and far from our shepherd. In a similar way, the grain on the stalk is vulnerable. It is out in the weather which can destroy it in many ways. Animals and birds could eat it and other people could steal it. But when it is brought in together with the rest of the crop in the farmer's barns, it is safe.

I believe in a very real sense the harvest is bringing converts together into a place of close relationship with Jesus as their bridegroom. I believe that movements, such as the International House of Prayer, which leads people into a unity of intimacy with God, are doing more to bring in the harvest than anything else in Christendom today.

Jesus saw the believing Jews as the harvest, which needed to be gathered. He could have gathered them together, but the leaders of the Jews were not willing to let Him. They wanted to keep the sheep for themselves and not surrender them to their King of Kings and Lord of Lords. They were the hirelings, while Jesus was the Shepherd, but they wouldn't surrender His sheep to Him. He wanted to gather them to Himself, while they wanted to keep them apart from Him for their own profit.

JESUS SENDS HIS LABORERS

Jesus then sent his disciples to the "lost" sheep of the house of Israel (Matthew 10). The word "lost" means hurting, wounded or destroyed. They were not the Gentiles; they were the people of faith, but they were not being taken care of by their leaders. They were being abused and spiritually injured and destroyed. Jesus told them not even to go to Samaria or the Gentiles at that point. They were to respond to His plea for harvesters by becoming the harvesters. They were to bring God's people the good news of the Kingdom of God, healing their sick and setting captives free.

It's clear to me that Jesus was asking His disciples to prepare the way for His coming to His people. They were to unite as one nation with one King. It was the Kingdom of God that they were to preach, and the Kingdom is simply the domain or rule of the King, who is Jesus. He wanted to gather His own Jewish people to Himself first, before going to the Samaritans and Gentiles.

Jesus is not just interested in getting people to believe in Him. He wants them to know Him intimately, and He wants them in unity with His other followers as part of His family and His bride. To Him, the harvest is bringing His family from everywhere in the world together in beautiful harmony in His house, loving Him and enjoying Him, just like the natural harvest is bringing all the grain into the farmer's barn.

USING PROPHETIC MINISTRY TO GATHER HIS HARVEST

With this expanded concept of harvest, we have an expanded application of the use of prophetic ministry for the harvest. If we think the harvest is simply evangelism, we will focus only on using prophecy to get people saved. But if we believe the harvest is also bringing God's children together into a beautiful unity of heart and soul to bring joy to our Heavenly Father and to our loving Bridegroom, then we will also focus on establishing and deepening an intimate, passionate love relationship with God and a unity that is powerful and strong.

When we visit church after church and group after group, we find believers who are just like the Jews that Jesus saw. Many of them have been wounded by religious leaders in their past. They still carry major wounds and need more than natural compassion and counseling to bring them into the place of intimacy with God.

What these people need is evidence that a supernatural God knows them, loves them and wants them in His close inner circle of intimacy. They are His sheep, but they are still scattered. They also need to be brought into a place of usefulness to Him. Just as the grain cannot be used for anything while it is still on the stalk, so the believer needs to be brought into a place of usefulness for the Master.

Being useful and valuable is the inner desire of every person. People who do not feel needed or loved are the sheep that are scattered. They are the ones that are not finding fulfillment. They don't know their destiny, and they don't believe their dreams will come true.

ENTER THE PROPHETIC MINISTRY

Kingdom-minded prophetic people can sense the hurt and pain of God's scattered sheep. They have an inner drive to transform the hurting and wounded sheep into intimate lovers of Jesus, mighty warriors and eager harvesters. The prophet's antennas catch the vibes coming from the scattered, lost sheep, and they begin to release a healing stream of words of life, renewal and restoration.

Words of knowledge of their hurts and pains quickly get the attention of the sad and hopeless, and before long they believe what they have always wanted to believe— that God actually does love them, wants them and He has a destiny and "usefulness" for them in His Kingdom.

They begin to fall in love with their King, and they allow themselves to be drawn into His house as part of His harvest. There they make themselves available there to do whatever He has for them to do. And one of the things they are willing to do is go where He sends them to look for other lost and scattered sheep that are still hurting like they were before they were found.

I have watched this scenario unfold hundreds or thousands of times, as I have ministered with my prophetic wife, Brenda. We have given words to several thousand people per year since the end of 1999. Many of those people were numbered among the lost and wounded sheep that were scattered without their Shepherd. They may have been in a church building, but they didn't feel like part of the family of God, nor did they have a close and intimate personal relationship with their King and Bridegroom.

But the affect of a word from the heart of their Heavenly Father has been totally amazing. We have seen so many totally transformed by the love of Jesus, which was released through prophetic ministry. Let me give you one special example.

A few years ago, after ministering in an Assembly of God Church in a Wednesday night service in Cortez, Colorado, we were invited to a home group by Leroy and Peggy Garcia later that week. Packed with about 25 people, we were busy ministering to each one, when their daughter walked into the house, coming home from work.

Rebekah Garcia was not really excited about us being there. We had invaded her space and she headed straight to her bedroom, but she had to walk through the living room to get there. Brenda's antennae were up and picking up some heavy vibes. She just had to minister to her. She quickly caught Rebekah's attention and began to speak to her with prophetic knowledge and compassion.

Rebekah broke and wept. Brenda ministered to her some more that night. Some months later we returned to Cortez. Rebekah was still struggling and didn't want to see Brenda, but again God reached into her heart. After three or four visits, Rebekah decided to go to Kansas City to do a six-month internship at the International House of Prayer.

She was so excited for months before she went, and while there she was powerfully transformed into an intimate and passionate lover of Jesus. She has now said, "Here am I, send me." We believe she will be powerfully used by God to raise up many other passionate lovers of Jesus.

Rebekah was one of the wounded, scattered sheep

that knew about Jesus, but was not gathered into His living room as part of His family in unity and love. She needed the prophetic ministry to harvest her and bring her into His beautiful house to be used by Him. She has and will always have a special place in our hearts.

I could go on to mention a young teen in Alberta, Canada, who was brought by her grandmother to a service where we were conducting a School of Prophetic Ministry. Brenda knew by the Holy Spirit that she had been brought against her own will and was suicidal. Brenda was drawn to her and began to reveal the secrets of her heart with a gentle, loving word from Jesus. She began to sob almost hysterically. She became a lover of Jesus and was brought into an awareness of His love for her.

The next time we came to Alberta, she brought a dozen or so members of her family to meet us and to receive ministry from us. It was amazing to see the beautiful smile on her face and the bubbling joy that flowed out from her. She was definitely a part of the harvest that Jesus sent us to bring in.

I could mention the older Korean lady in Illinois that Brenda ministered to through an interpreter, telling her that God knew about her loneliness and other emotional attacks she had been going through. She also wept profusely. After the word she also confessed to being depressed and suicidal.

The next time we saw her was after a church service.

She saw us and, not able to speak much English, she hopped up and down and repeated one word, "Happy, Happy, Happy!!!" What she was communicating is that she was no longer isolated from the joy of serving God with all her heart. Rather, she was filled with passion and joy and available for the master to use. The last we heard, she was actively serving the Lord in a Korean church.

As Jesus said, "The harvest is ripe." It's time to use the harvesting tool called prophetic ministry to bring in the whole harvest, both the unbelievers, who just need more evidence to convince them; and the believers, who need the healing warmth of Jesus to bring them into His House of Intimacy and Joy.

Chapter Six

Preparation for Prophetic Ministry

THE PROPHETIC GIFT OR MINISTRY IS THE ONLY ONE MEN-
TIONED in each of the four major lists of gifts and ministries. Each of these lists have instructions preceding
and/or following them. These instructions are very
valuable and insightful when it comes to preparation
for prophetic ministry.

God has given us an awesome manual for the use
of His power tools. Reading and studying His manual
will keep us from all kinds of problems when we try to
work with these tools. So many people fail to read the
manual and the results can often be destructive or even
catastrophic.

The instructions in our manual are not so much what
we might look for, like how do you interpret dreams
and visions, or how do you get dreams and visions in
the first place? The instructions are more important than

that. They include a number of very crucial "attitude checks." Let's look at them briefly.

Please don't skip, skim or ignore these instructions, like so many men and women have done before they shipwrecked their ministries. Remembering and following these instructions can make the difference between the success or failure to bring in the harvest and please the Master.

1. Be a Living Sacrifice

Romans 12:1 exhorts us to present ourselves to God as a living sacrifice. This is not an option for those who would bring in the Master's harvest. We must decide whose side we are on—ours or His. If we don't surrender our will, our pride, our ambition and our flesh in general, we will do more harm than good trying to work alongside other harvesters.

2. Renew Your Mind

Romans 12:2 commands us not to be conformed to this world, but to be transformed by the renewing of our minds. The word for renewing is from the word for renovation. Our natural and humanistically-programmed mind needs an extreme makeover. This can happen only by a Godly "brain-washing" with the Word and the Holy Spirit.

3. Think Soberly—Be Humble

Romans 12:3 declares that we should not think of ourselves more highly than we ought to think, but to think soberly. We are not to think of ourselves as nobodies or insignificant, but neither should we think that we are more important than other members of His body.

A drunken person thinks he can take a 30 mph curve at 75. A sober person has better discernment of his abilities and doesn't endanger himself and others with reckless behavior. Many prophetic people have done great damage by thinking that they don't need to be accountable to anyone. They believe that everything they think or say comes from God. The enemy has a great time bringing them and many others down through their pride.

4. We Are All Unique and Our Gifts Are Different

Although all the gifts come from the same Holy Spirit, I Corinthians 12:2-6 tells us that:

"There are diversities of gifts, but the same Spirit. There are differences of ministries, but the same Lord. And there are diversities of activities, but it is the same God who works all in all."

None of us are carbon copies of anyone else. All of us have a unique combination of personality traits and spiritual gifts. Even when two people have the same gift, they will not function exactly alike. Every gift is colored and flavored by the personality and other gifts of the person that it flows through.

All Christians with the Holy Spirit flowing through them are handcrafted and gifted with special care by the Creator. We are uniquely designed for a special calling and mission in life. No one is left out as we are about to prove.

5. Remember the "Each One" Principle

Every time spiritual gifts are mentioned in the New Testament, we read something in the context about the fact that each one has been given gifts by the Holy Spirit. In fact there are seven New Testament Scriptures with the phrase "each one."

I Corinthians 12 contains what I called a "7-11 Super Sandwich." Verses 8, 9 and 10 list nine spiritual gifts. Both verse 7 and verse 11 contain the phrase "each one." The gifts are the meat and the "each one's" are the bread. Verse 7 says:

"But the manifestation of the Spirit is given to EACH ONE for the profit of all."

Verse 11 says:

"But one and the same Spirit works all these things, distributing to EACH ONE individually as He wills."

The most important point about the "each one's" is that no one can say they don't have a spiritual ministry. The other important point is that we should not feel superior to others when we discover how to use spiritual gifts. We were all given gifts and we have a responsibility to use them for the benefit of everyone else and not for our own personal advantage.

My personal favorite verse of all those relating to each one having spiritual gifts is I Peter 4:10.

"As each one has received a gift, minister it to one another, as good stewards of the manifold grace of God."

This verse begins with the assumption that we know that we have received a gift. The second point is that we are commanded to serve one another with this gift. Again it is made clear that the gift was not given to us for personal advantage but to serve others.

The next important point from this verse is that when you serve one another with your gift or gifts, you are being a good steward of God's grace. If we are thankful for God's grace and value it as precious, we should be good stewards of that grace.

The amazing thing is how much sense it makes when you know the Greek words for "grace" and "gift."

In the Greek, the word "grace" in the Greek is "Charis," and the word for "gift" is "Charisma." Since the gift is a thing of grace, if we neglect to use this "grace thing" to serve each other, we are not being good stewards of God's grace.

When we think of stewardship we usually think of finances, but here is a clear declaration that God wants us to be good stewards of spiritual gifts.

A final important point gained from this verse is that God's grace is "manifold," or plentiful or generous. In other words, God gave us an abundant supply of this grace to operate these gifts. The gifts are not given with a stingy or reluctant attitude. They are given freely. We have all freely received, and we need to give freely of our gifts to others.

6. We Are All Members of His Body—The Body of Christ

Sandwiched between two lists of spiritual gifts and ministries in I Corinthians 12, is an extensive discussion of the body of Christ. The importance of this discussion cannot be overestimated. The meat of this chapter clearly implies that the gifts and ministries given to us by God give us our function and position in the body of Christ.

Let's first deal with the expression, "body of Christ." This has become too much of a cliché to most of us, so let's think about what it really is saying. The body of Christ is not just people in the church. The body of Christ IS actually the body of Christ—that is the body that the Christ possesses and lives in on this earth.

The point is: It is HIS body. It is not about us and what we need or want to accomplish. It is about HIM and the work that HE wants to accomplish. Just as my body serves me to do the work I want to accomplish, so His body was designed to do the work He wants to accomplish.

The problem is that while Jesus had a physical body on the earth that served Him faithfully and did His every bidding, today He has a body composed of parts that seem to have their own mind and will. His earthly body of two thousand years ago had all its members working together in harmony, but today, His earthly body is composed of many parts which are totally disconnected from each other and unwilling to work together for the good of the whole body and the desires of the Head.

Another significant point is that the New Testament never uses the term, "The body of Jesus." I used to use that term to make the point more clear. But the term used by Paul is the "body of Christ." We are not just the body of the man, Jesus, on the earth. We are the body of the Christ, the "Anointed One." In and through this body, composed of redeemed human beings, there flows the same anointing that Jesus received from the Holy Spirit for His earthly ministry.

When we are able to function in the unity and harmony that Jesus had in His first earthly body, and then again in the early Jerusalem church, we will see the great and awesome things that Jesus and the early church saw. The body of Christ, the Anointed One, must pursue the unity that will release the flow of that anointing again.

7. Passionately Desire to Prophesy

I Corinthians 14 gives us a detailed discussion of the gift of prophecy. The first verse goes like this:

"Pursue Love, and desire spiritual gifts, but especially that you may prophesy."

The second to the last verse of the chapter concludes the discussion:

"Therefore brethren, desire earnestly to prophesy and do not forbid to speak with tongues."

From start to finish this chapter discusses the value

of prophecy, especially how it is superior to the gift of tongues, unless the tongues are interpreted or understood. Both the introduction and the conclusion of this chapter tell us that God wants us to have and use this gift. Paul also tells us in verse 31:

> *"For you can all prophesy one by one, that all may learn and all may be encouraged."*

It is so important to realize that we can prophesy and God wants us to desire this gift.

8. Pursue Excellence in Edification of His Body

We are often told to pursue excellence in everything we do. Paul gave us one very important area in which to pursue excellence. In I Corinthians 14:12, he instructed the church:

> *"Even so you, since you are zealous for spiritual gifts, let it be for the edification of the church, that you seek to excel."*

I have yet to see a book written or hear a sermon on the subject, "How to edify." And yet Paul specifically mentioned that we should seek to excel in this area. But it is clear that Paul was instructing us to edify through prophetic words that we give to one another.

The whole chapter is talking about prophecy, and the whole chapter is also talking about edifying or building up the body of Christ. So many Christians think that they have been called to be building inspectors instead of builders. But the cry of God is that we would all be builders. He will be the building inspector and He will speak to His leaders.

My advice for those who have contributed to the "Paralysis of Analysis" by becoming building inspectors, is that if you don't trust God to answer your prayers to correct and redirect your leaders when they are going astray, then you need to follow other leaders. Or you need to develop your own faith and prayer life to the point where you believe God is big enough to change your leaders without you having to talk negatively with other members about them.

9. Walk Worthy of Your Calling

Moving on to Ephesians 4:1, the introduction to the Five-Fold Ministries, we find some very important instructions under the heading, "Walk Worthy." One might think that walking worthy of a high calling might focus on holding one's head high and enjoying the exalted position. Instead, Paul directs us, including those with these exalted ministries, to keep a very humble profile. The particular instructions are discussed below.

Humility

The first instruction is to walk worthy of your calling with all "lowliness and gentleness." This pictures humility of heart and is the foundational attitude that every servant of the Lord must possess. We remember that Jesus said, that the greatest among us is the servant of all.

Love With Longsuffering

Paul goes on to add that to walk worthy of our high calling, we need to be longsuffering and ready to bear with one another in love. The only way to walk worthy of our high calling is with the mind and attitude of Jesus who was filled with the same Holy Spirit, who is available to us also.

Through the Spirit of Love, we can have patience for those who mess up and for those whose flesh offends us. Longsuffering is a fruit of the Holy Spirit and we need this fruit frequently when we are working as part of a team, especially in leadership positions.

Guarding the Unity of the Spirit

Walking worthy of our divine calling also involves being guardians of the Unity of the Holy Spirit in the bond of peace. The real meaning of the sentence in the Greek is: *Make haste, give diligence and make every effort to guard or protect from being stolen, by keeping your eyes on the unity of the Spirit.*

I often say that this is one of the least kept commandments in the Bible. We have not as the people of God guarded this precious gift that the early church once enjoyed to an amazing level. We have allowed the enemy to steal us blind in so many ways. Unity has so often been sacrificed or exchanged for the desire to be "right."

My firm conviction, however, is that this wonderful and powerful commodity will be restored to us in order that we might be found able to bring in the Master's great and final harvest of souls. The unity of the early church will be equaled and exceeded before the return of Jesus to this earth.

Not everyone who claims today to be a Christian will be a part of this unity, but those who are truly committed to Jesus will be part of something so big and beautiful and powerful, that millions of souls will be worshipping and serving God together in spirit and truth. The love for one another will flow and it will be expressed through many practical acts of kindness.

I have experienced a foretaste of this unity a few times, mostly on the mission field, where God was releasing His healing and miracle power. It is interesting that some of the phenomena in the church, that have seemingly separated it into opposing camps, such as healing and renewal manifestations, have actually produced the most tangible unity among those who have abandoned their pride to seek after Jesus with all their hearts.

The greatest tangible unity I have ever experienced was in Argentina in 1973. As soon as the prophetic and healing ministry began to explode through my mentor, Elmer Burnette, pastors who had been feuding were immediately reconciled and the love among everyone began to manifest like I had never seen before. It was one of the most exciting times of my life.

Chapter Seven

Multiplying Prophetic Ministry for the Harvest

As we have discussed earlier, prophetic ministry is useful in the harvest in two distinct ways. The first is to encourage the workers and activate them to get into the harvest field themselves. The second is to minister to those who don't know Christ by revealing to them that God knows them and loves them and has a purpose and plan for their lives.

But as Jesus said, "The harvest is plentiful, but the laborers are few." Those gifted in prophetic ministry are far too few, and we must accelerate the training and equipping of many more prophets. We must have the same passion as Paul, who gave us the exhortation to desire earnestly to prophesy, and Moses, who said in Numbers 11:29:

"Oh that all the Lord's people were prophets, and that the Lord would put His Spirit upon them."

Moses had no fear of competition or of over-saturating the congregation with prophetic ministers. I don't think we should either — especially with the need for workers in the great harvest of the last days.

I do sincerely believe that the harvest depends a lot on prophetic ministry and that it must be done correctly. What the church and the world have seen in the past has been largely a turn-off to many, who could see through the self-serving motives of those proclaiming themselves as prophets. We must change the perception that people have of the prophet and prophetic ministry.

There are some important steps to follow if we are to prepare for the harvest with the powerful tool of Prophetic Ministry:

WE MUST GO TO GREAT LENGTHS TO AVOID THE PERCEPTION THAT WE ARE SEEKING FINANCIAL GAIN

The prophet deserves financial support as much as any other ministry, such as pastor. I discussed the financing of the five-fold ministry in my book, "Folding Five Ministries into One Powerful Team." I demonstrated both the strengths and weaknesses in our present church culture.

Because ministries, such as itinerants, who depend entirely on offerings for their support, are often motivated to some level of manipulation and excess focus on finances, many people have a problem with the way itinerant ministries go after finances, especially those ministries who are more charismatic. Prophetic ministries and other itinerant ministries need support as well, but to compensate for the negative perception, we must develop a greater level of faith in God for our finances.

And learning to trust God for finances should be a natural for someone called into a prophetic ministry. We accepted that life-style many years ago and have seen God act powerfully on our behalf. We have had periods of testing in this area, but we always knew that God was stretching us for a purpose and keeping us humble. The periods of testing always come to an end and His blessings begin to pour out on us again to meet our needs.

PROPHETIC MINISTRY MUST EMPHASIZE THAT IT'S NOT ABOUT THE PROPHET

There is a powerful spirit of resistance to the implied claim of spiritual superiority or spiritual authority that prophetic people have allowed to exist or even encouraged and perpetuated in their meetings. Men and women with a strong prophetic anointing have been prone to enjoy the admiration and honor that people want to give to them.

Pretty soon there is more focus on the prophet than the message he or she is bringing. The admiration and honor often translate into increased finances, which are always needed by ministries with a vision for growth and increase. Thus it's hard to resist that place of enjoying the honor and admiration. And it's also hard to resist the temptation to use that honor and admiration for personal advantage and gain.

But resist it we must, if we want Jesus to be exalted. We must be forerunners, like John the Baptist, who said, "He must increase, but I must decrease." We must hide ourselves behind the cross and promote Jesus and His Kingdom.

I clearly remember my first missionary trip to Argentina in 1973. My mentor, Elmer Burnette, was being used powerfully by God. During the six glorious weeks, we saw hundreds of miracles, awesome intense worship and the salvation of over one thousand souls.

Elmer was moving in a powerful prophetic anointing, and he was calling out healings in different parts of the audience. But there were several times, after he had emphasized that it was Jesus and not him doing the miracles, when he had to stop and say something like this: "The Holy Spirit is showing me that people are looking at a man rather than Jesus. He won't do any more miracles if we don't take our eyes off man."

When this sunk into the minds and hearts of the hundreds of people attending, Elmer would go on and administrate the release of God's healing and prophetic anointing on the people. The lasting results included five new churches, with a combined total of over 1,000 members in the cities where we had ministered in those six glorious weeks.

PROPHETIC PEOPLE MUST HAVE A KINGDOM-FIRST MENTALITY

Having a Kingdom-first mentality is crucial for the harvest. If we focus on building our ministry, we will often sacrifice Kingdom gains to protect our own little kingdom. It plays out in so many small ways, but it adds up to big losses for God's Kingdom. For more insight, see the last chapter of my previous book, "With Me," where I talk about the "local" church.

This need to be a "Kingdom First" people is especially critical when it relates to prophetic ministry and to young people. Since prophetic ministry is such a powerful tool, if we direct its focus on building our ministry, we will miss powerful opportunities to build the Kingdom of God.

The youth of today are going to be used to expand the Kingdom of God like no previous generation. Therefore, it is critical that we don't hold them back, or try to use them to build our own kingdoms, when they have a call to the nations and not just our local ministry.

What I mean by a Kingdom-first mentality is a perspective that says, "If I can sacrifice my own desires and ambitions to do something to bless God's Kingdom, I will gladly do it." One simple example would be letting go of a young person who is a major blessing to our ministry in leading worship, for example. He or she may desire to take more training or take a trip to a mission field, but we have no one to replace him or her. Our natural tendency would be to counsel the worship leader to stay until God provides a replacement. The flesh might even want to invoke a "prophetic word" to make it more convincing. But if we let them go, they would take their gifting to a new level and be better prepared to go to the ends of the earth to bring in the greater harvest.

The wonderful thing about doing what is right is that Jesus promised that if we sought first His Kingdom and His righteousness all the things we needed would be added to us. (Matthew 6:33). If we release one worship leader, it might cause two brand new worship leaders to be raised up, or even worship teams, which would bring the worship in our own ministry to a new level. Or God may send us someone even more anointed than the first.

WE MUST MENTOR AND TRAIN AS MANY PROPHETIC PEOPLE AS POSSIBLE

While we are learning to get it right and developing our ability to hear God's voice, we must also be aware that there are many Christians all around us who are still totally uninformed or undeveloped in their own prophetic giftings. God is looking for someone who will help them understand His call on their lives and His desire to use them in prophetic ministry.

We have done a little mentoring as we have moved from place to place, but we are taking mentoring to a much more serious level in these days, especially with the youth who are so ready and eager to get started touching other people's lives. On our present journey we have seen many young people take their prophetic and healing ministries to a brand new level. It has been truly amazing to observe.

If we had been content to just do what we could do to minister to as many people as possible by ourselves, we would have robbed some of the people we came to minister to, and we would have robbed the young apprentices of an opportunity to develop their gifts for the Kingdom. It should be stated that we were so blessed to have an awesome group of young people who were already very much sold out to God and wanted to know and exalt God more than they wanted a ministry to feel good or boast about.

I believe that every Christian should move quickly from being a follower only, to being a follower and a leader at the same time. We can learn from our mentors, while being a mentor of others. We know Paul was still mentoring and teaching Timothy, through letters, while

Timothy was already considered an apostle and leading churches as a young man.

One of the most exciting things that is happening right now under our noses is watching the older teens begin to mentor the younger teens. Our younger sons and their friends minister in a house of prayer in Illinois. We encouraged them to mentor the younger teens that they knew and bring them into the worship and prayer ministry. I felt that they should each reproduce several more worshippers to expand the worship ministry into new dimensions and to replace themselves when they moved on.

The seventeen and eighteen-year olds have been mentoring the thirteen to fifteen year olds, and I believe it has just begun. And we find that kids learn from other kids much faster than they learn from adults. The younger ones already admire the older teens, and they love having the attention of the older kids who would normally shut them out of their little circle.

We also have seen the older adult generation learning from us and other ministries that would give them opportunities to learn and practice. God led us in some interesting ways to bring people together in such a way that they could develop their prophetic giftings, which had been lying dormant for some time.

One of the first experiences with this was in Las Vegas, where we wanted to do some street and park ministry to bikers and hurting people in the area. We invited people from different parts of the country. A dozen people showed up from Alberta, Canada, a dozen from Chicago, Illinois and a dozen from Dallas, Texas. One young man came from Idaho and led worship for us.

Some of our plans did not work out the way we expected, but a powerful and lasting result of the meetings was that our team began to minister to each other. Prophetic giftings were released there in unprecedented ways. From that beginning, most of the team members learned to exercise their spiritual senses by learning to listen to words from the Holy Spirit, as well as to see visions. Of course, they would then speak out what they were receiving, in order to help someone else.

Mentoring is not just having an assistant to build your own ministry; it is the most effective and powerful way to raise up ministries. It is true that people learn by helping and serving, but the heart of the mentor must be to prepare the student to move on to greater things. The mentor should be ready to release the student as soon as he will benefit from another assignment in the Kingdom of God.

Some people will find total fulfillment in serving a senior pastor or evangelist, but we as leaders must be careful that we don't squelch a helper's ministry by keeping him or her under our shadow to make us look good. These are things that we won't do consciously, but we should be willing to ask God to search our hearts when it comes to assistants or associates.

TIPS ON MENTORING

1. Pray about people who want you to mentor them. Only commit yourself to the ones that you believe God has spoken to you about. Mentoring is something that can drain you of a lot of your time and energy. It is critical that we mentor the ones God has for us.

2. Be honest with your trainees or disciples. Be humble and let them know you have messed up or failed many times. A proud person makes a very poor mentor. Be ready to be an example to them by apologizing for your mistakes, oversights and lack of sensitivity, etc.

   If you are aware of the fact that you were not totally Christ-like in your attitude or behavior in front of them, let them know that you realize the error of what you have done, and that you are sorry for being a poor example. They will be much more willing to follow you and serve you if you are real and humble.

3. Take time to ask them what they have been learning and what they see that could be improved upon in your own ministry. Ask them about their fears and failures. Encourage them to keep pressing in and not quitting. We must all go through some dark valleys before we

come out strong and effective on the other side.

4. Keep seeking more clarity in understanding the giftings and callings of your students. Give them opportunities to develop different gifts to see if they will suddenly blossom in one particular ministry. Some have great latent musical and worship talents, but they have never been given much opportunity to develop them. Others are highly prophetic, but have never stepped out. Some have great healing gifts, but have not been pushed to use them and don't really know what they have in their own hands.

5. Observe or discern by the Holy Spirit the leadership giftings in your students and be quick to give opportunities for them to take charge of things. You have to take some risks or you will not promote the development that they need. They can learn from their mistakes, and if you demonstrate an example of humility, they will be willing to listen to your correction and advice.

TIPS FOR THOSE LOOKING FOR MENTORS

If you are one of the multitudes of believers looking for someone to help you develop your gifts and ministries to fulfill your destiny, you have a tough task ahead of you. There are many ministries but few mentors willing to take time to develop your ministry.

1. First of all, determine that whether you find a human mentor or not who will teach and train you, you will be discipled (disciplined) by the Holy Spirit and the Word of God. But do earnestly seek the Lord for the person that God may have for you to help you develop your gifts for His Kingdom's sake. Then commit yourself to helping mentor others as soon as you are ready, whether you find someone to mentor you or not.

2. When you find someone you respect who is willing to invest time in you, appreciate every moment and insight that he or she shares with you. Generally, people who have something to offer you as far as mentoring is concerned are usually people who already have a full plate and not enough time for their families and quiet times for themselves. They will serve you because they see something special in you and want the joy of seeing you develop as a spiritual son or daughter, but it will still cost them something. Don't forget to show your thanks and honor them for it. It will make them want to serve you even more.

3. Be patient with the weaknesses of your mentor, which you will see before too long. They may lack patience or wisdom in certain areas. They may not be sensitive to your tender heart and can hurt your feelings without realizing it. Prophetic people, especially, can be insensitive, although others, who are more pastoral, like my wife, can be extremely sensitive. The key is to remember that although they may have dynamic ministries, they are still very human. I have also noticed that the strongest ministries often have strong corresponding character weaknesses. Pray for them as they serve you and as you serve them.

4. Be hungry for knowledge and opportunities to learn and grow. Be teachable and moldable. The greater desire you manifest, the more your mentor will want to spend time with you.

5. Be a servant. Elisha was known as the one who poured water on the hands of Elijah. That was the job of a servant. Look for ways to serve your mentor and do everything you can to make his or her ministry successful. Your faithful service, even when things are not fun, will open doors for you. And in the end you can ask for a double portion of your mentor's ministry.

FINE TUNING FOR THE HARVEST

It's time to activate our own ministries and prepare to activate and mentor others. The harvest is so ripe. Revival is in full swing in many nations. It has already been birthed in our western world and is growing quickly.

God is preparing the finances and the labor force for an accelerated harvest. We are seeing and hearing about many exciting things in these days. Prophets have spoken repeatedly about the transfer of wealth from the nations to the Kingdom. They also speak of tremendous gatherings in stadiums where unknown young people are administrating incredible miracles and revival.

But God won't do it without our cooperation. And what He wants us to do is what He commanded in I Corinthians 14. He wants us to desire earnestly to prophesy. He wants us to seek to excel in edifying or building up the body of Christ, so Jesus can work through an anointed and strong body again.

We need to remember that prophetic ministry is a major forerunner of the greater miracles. It is also a powerful tool in itself to bring people to faith. And then we need to remember that the harvest is more than getting people saved. It also includes bringing them into the Father's house where they feel loved and can receive their special assignment from their Father.

And finally, let's not forget to help as many people

as possible in fulfilling their destinyies. They need to be told and reminded often how much God loves them and what a great plan He has for their lives. They need repeated confirmation that He will be with them and bring them into victory over every attack of the enemy.

If we follow the example of Jesus and learn to listen to the Heavenly Father's voice, we will be able to carry His voice to those who need help hearing it.

Let me finish this short book with one more Scripture verse. We referred to I Peter 4:10 earlier. We didn't mention verse 11, which is a great follow-up verse and a great Scripture with which to end this study of prophetic ministry and the harvest.

I Peter 4:11 reads like this:

"If anyone speaks, let him speak as the oracles of God. If anyone ministers, let him do it as with the ability which God supplies, that in all things God may be glorified through Jesus Christ, to whom belong the glory and the dominion forever and ever. Amen."

The first part of the verse is pretty strong. We are not to speak about our own ideas, but actually speak as the oracles of God. That is a pretty tough command to obey. It would really require us to "walk in the Spirit" and "pray without ceasing."

The important point for our study is that God does expect us to speak for Him. This implies that we have the capacity to hear His voice and to speak His words.

The conclusion of the verse is also important. All the honor and glory must go to God. Using the gifts and tools which He has given us are the best way to give Him the glory. It should be clear to us and our hearers that when something supernatural takes place, it is because a supernatural Being is involved and He will receive the glory.

The harvest is ripe! He has chosen you and me to bring it in. Furthermore, He has given us some incredible tools. We need to learn how to use them, and then we need to go after the harvest with these tools.

We CAN do it and we MUST do it! As God told Ezekiel, "Son of man, prophesy to the dry bones." Even though our audience may seem cold and dry, they won't be as cold and dry as Ezekiel's dry bones.

So let's prophesy as He commanded us, and bring the harvest to our Lord and Master for His own awesome and wonderful plan and purpose. Amen!

Ben R. Peters

With over 40 years of ministry experience, Ben Peters with his wife, Brenda, have been called to an international apostolic ministry of equipping and activating others. As founders and directors of Open Heart Ministries, Ben and Brenda have ministered to tens of thousands with teaching and prophetic ministry. The result is that many have been saved, healed, delivered and activated into powerful ministries of their own.

Ben has been given significant insights for the body of Christ and has written fourteen books in the past ten years, since beginning a full-time itinerant ministry. His passions and insights include unity in the body of Christ, accessing the glory of God, five-fold team ministry, prophetic ministry, and signs and wonders for the world-wide harvest.

Kingdom Sending Center
P.O. Box 25
Genoa, IL 60135

www.KingdomSendingCenter.org
ben.peters@kingdomsendingcenter.org

Made in the USA
San Bernardino, CA
28 August 2017